Lyn is a nutritional therapist who believes that educating people about how our bodies work is the first step towards changing how we think about food. Armed with know-how and simple tips, we can change what comfort and convenience food means to us. With the hindsight acquired from her own health issues which led her to study nutrition, she understands that focusing on your health has the power to be the catalyst to enhance or change your life for the better.

Lyn Sharkey

Fantastic Food
& Why to Eat It!

Commentary by Nathan Sherlock

AUSTIN MACAULEY PUBLISHERS™
LONDON * CAMBRIDGE * NEW YORK * SHARJAH

Copyright © Lyn Sharkey 2023

The right of Lyn Sharkey to be identified as author of this work has been asserted in accordance with sections 77 and 78 of the Copyright, Designs and Patents Act 1988.

Commentary © Nathan Sherlock 2023

All rights reserved. No part of this publication may be reproduced, stored in a retrieval system, or transmitted in any form or by any means, electronic, mechanical, photocopying, recording, or otherwise, without the prior permission of the publishers.

Any person who commits any unauthorised act in relation to this publication may be liable to criminal prosecution and civil claims for damages.

A CIP catalogue record for this title is available from the British Library.

ISBN 9781398496835 (Paperback)
ISBN 9781398496842 (Hardback)
ISBN 9781398496866 (ePub e-book)

www.austinmacauley.com

First Published 2023
Austin Macauley Publishers Ltd®
1 Canada Square
Canary Wharf
London
E14 5AA

Acknowledgements

I would like to thank my husband, Dessie, and our amazing extended family for always being so encouraging, and quite simply kind and wonderful people. I would also like to thank my clients who I learn so much from, and finally the students in the schools I have visited for asking such great questions and for being interested (for the most part) in how food can help them to feel well.

Lyn x

I would like to thank my "godmum" and Aunty Lyn for teaching me about food and including me in the book. My mum and dad for making sure I have the right food to eat and Austin Macauley Publishers for publishing Lyn's book.

Nathan

I would like to thank my nephew, Nathan, for his invaluable help with this book and the lovely staff of Austin Macauley Publishers for their encouragement, help and guidance along this journey to publish our book, which we hope will be a resource for you to learn how to invest in your own health.

Hey Kiddo!

How are you today? We are very grateful that you are reading our book, so thank you so much! We are super excited to tell you about how healthy food can help you in so many ways to do, be and feel your best. In other words...

- To **DO** everything **you** want to do

- To **BE** the best you can be

- To **FEEL** in a better mood

We all want to have energy so that we can be fun and learn more about things that we are interested in, right?

You are probably all very familiar with meat, chicken and chips, and maybe even a little pizza and hamburger. So, no need to try to persuade you to eat those!!! In this book, we would like to encourage you to eat some more vegetables and other natural or whole foods that you might not eat so often.

When food is changed too much (or processed), your body gets confused and doesn't know where the food should go or what it is supposed to do with it – kind of like if your football team were out on the pitch ready to play a match and instead of being given a football, they were given a ping-pong ball! How on earth would you play a good game of football with a ping-pong ball? 🤸

We hope that you might be willing to add some of these foods into your meals, if you don't already, and that you will also learn a little about how your amazing body works!

First, though, we would like to introduce ourselves to you.🤗

Lyn

Hi – I'm Lyn, and I am Nathan's aunt and godmother, so that makes him both my nephew and godson – my godphew! I am a **nutritional therapist** (aka I know about food) and LOVE FOOD. I especially love natural food, because it gives me the energy I need to do everything that I want to do. It also makes me feel happier and stronger.

I get so excited talking about it to anyone that will listen, because it means that we can actually DO something every day to help ourselves feel healthier and happier. When you are eating healthily, you can eat loads as well – YESSS!

Anyway, before I get carried away talking about all of the yummy things you could eat to support your health, let me introduce you to my godphew (and one of my best buds)

Nathan

Hi, my name is Nathan and I am 11 years old! I don't always eat as healthy as Lyn, but I'm helping her with this book to learn more about healthy foods. Children nearly always ask for fast food like, for example, chicken nuggets, chips and pizza and takeaways like that, but that isn't right. Yes, of course, it's okay to have them every now and then, just not ALL of the time.

Food can help me stay fit for my sports. So, I can't wait to find out why I should eat healthier food!

About Our Book

We thought that we would like the book to be a bit challenging for all of you clever kids out there, and hopefully some fun as well. Parts of the book are like a workbook, so you will read a chapter and then do a quiz at the end. If you use a pencil, you can rub out your answers when you are finished and share the book with a friend, or even take the quizzes again and again (repeating information is the best way to learn, after all). Let the challenge begin...

ok let's go.

So, how does our body work?

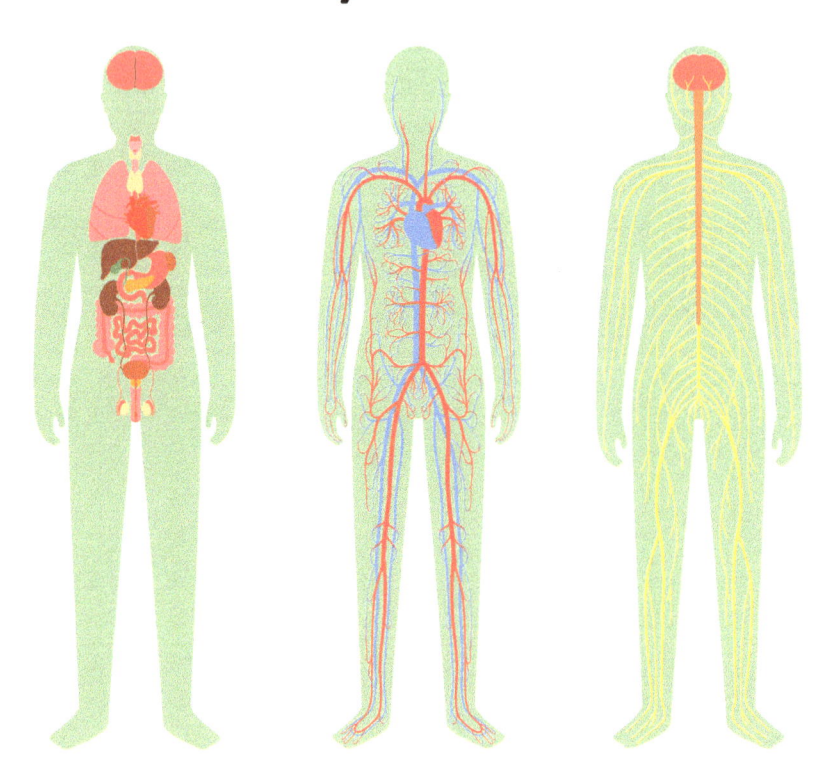

A Little Bit of Biology

To begin with, we thought that you might like to know a little bit about how your body works, so that you can really understand why we need to eat healthy food.

We are made up of billions (yes, that is billions) of tiny cells, and they all contain a little battery in the middle called mitochondria (Mite-O-Kon-Dree-E-A) which makes our energy.

A group of cells that are like each other get together and form tissue (so tissue is a group of cells)

Then a group of tissue gets together and forms our muscles, bones, skin and organs. By the way, organs are not like a mouth organ or a piano organ 😜. The organs in our body are our heart, lungs, liver, kidneys, tummy, skin and even our brain.

Our body organs form systems, and then all of these systems together form our body.

So, I guess the cells would be like a football player, the tissue would be like a team of football players, the organs would be like a league of teams (e.g. the Premier League), and the body would be like all different types of sports leagues together – the whole world of sport! They all work together to help you do what you need to do in a day 😊.

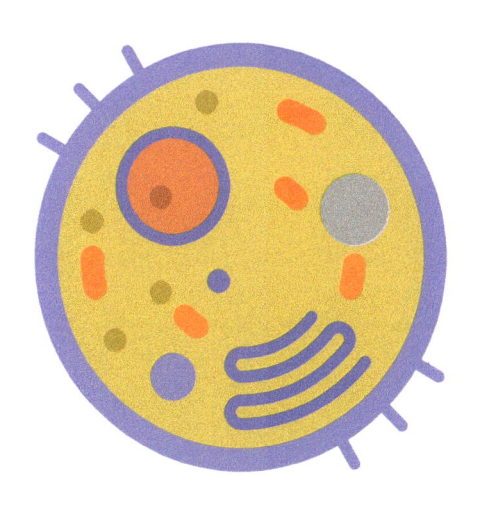

> **NATHAN SAYS:**
> *Isn't it amazing that our muscles are made up of tiny little cells!!!*

Quick Quiz...

Without looking at the last page, can you name 3 organs in our body and mark where you think they are on the drawing?

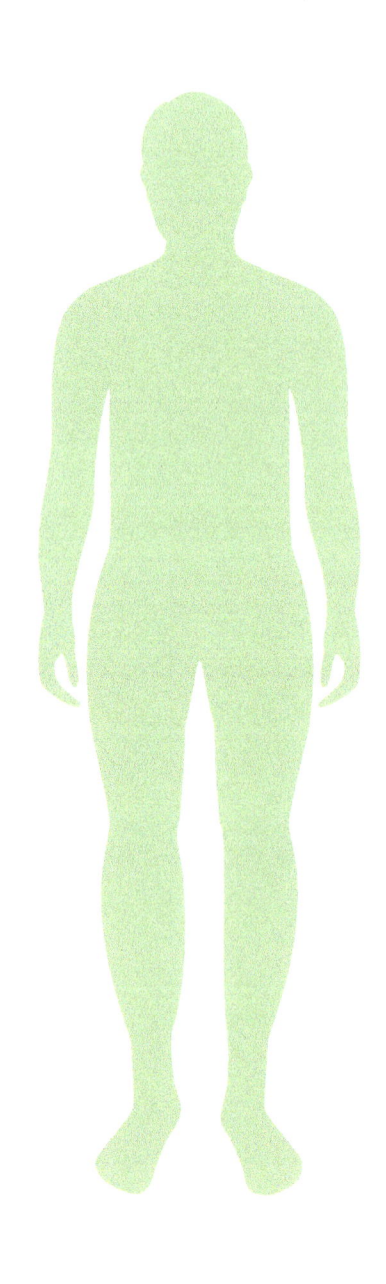

_____

_____

_____

Can you guess one thing that each organ does? Why don't you have a guess and then check back later to see if you were right...

Heart _____

Lungs _____

Liver _____

Kidneys _____

Brain _____

Bladder _____

Stomach _____

Intestine _____

> **NATHAN SAYS:**
> *Oh, so close on that one! I got about half of them right. Good luck!*

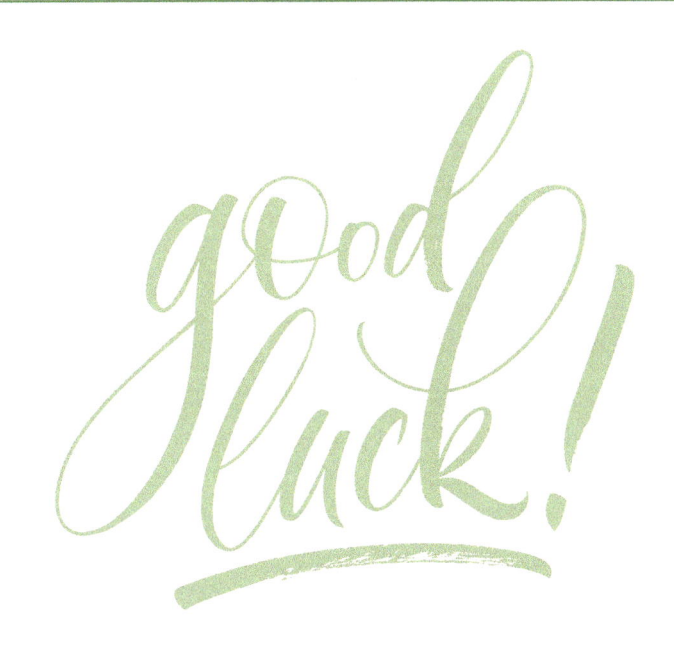

good luck!

Human Body with Organs

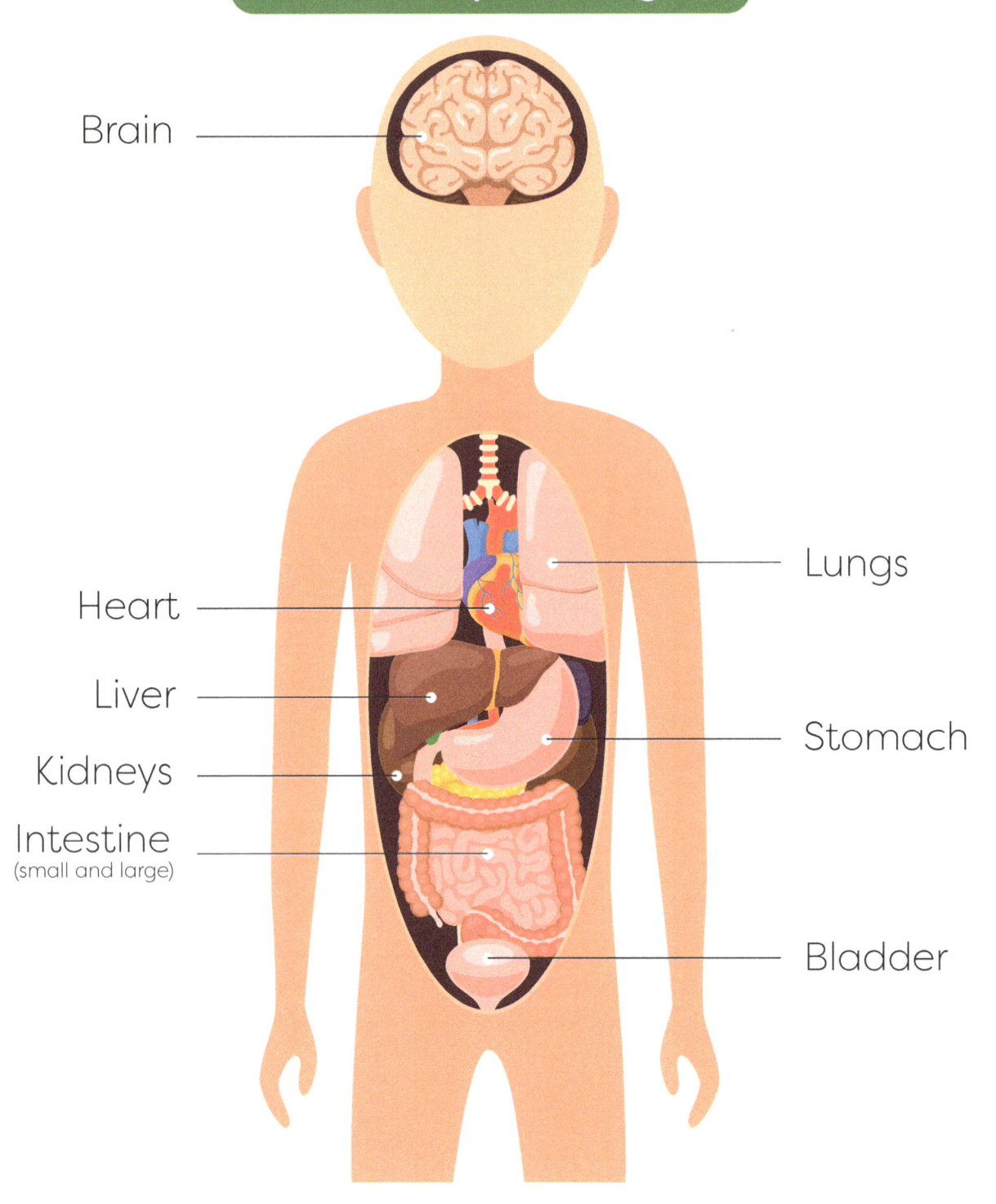

- Brain
- Heart
- Liver
- Kidneys
- Intestine (small and large)
- Lungs
- Stomach
- Bladder

Just a few things that our organs do...

Brain

Our brain is like a teacher – it controls the whole class!

It is quite amazing and tells our muscles to move when they need to. It happens so fast that we wouldn't even know it is happening!

It also tells them how to move and in what order (this helps when we are trying to move two muscles at the same time, like running and bouncing a ball) – that is called co-ordination (Ko-ord-in-ay-shun).

The brain makes sense of what we hear, see, feel, touch and smell, so that we can put a name on these things and understand them.

It helps us to talk (except when we are not supposed to, in class, of course 😜 – remember the brainy teacher!!)

Our brain holds our memories, like the last time we had a really good laugh with a friend or family.

Lungs

We have two lungs, and they take oxygen from the air that we breathe into our body, because all of our cells need oxygen.

Then, they exhale, or breathe out, carbon dioxide because this was also in the air, mixed in with the oxygen, but we don't need to keep it.

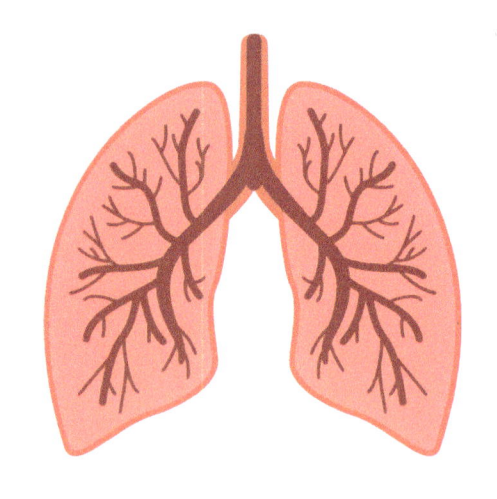

Liver

Our liver is a very busy organ and carries out lots of jobs. These are just a few of the big ones which help us to stay healthy.

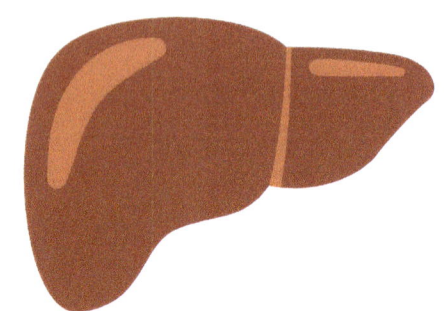

Firstly, it cleans our blood by separating the things that are good for our health and the things that we don't need. The good things are left in our blood and delivered to the cells that need them, and the other useless things that we don't need are peed or pooped out.

It makes bile, a fluid which breaks down fats in our food, so that we can handle them. It also makes things which help us to stop bleeding when we get a cut – very handy if you fall over a lot playing sports!

Our liver helps to keep our blood sugar balanced, so we need to help out by not putting too much pressure on it and having TOO much sugar!!

It also keeps nutrients and energy in a store, ready to put back into our blood when we need them.

Kidneys

We have two kidneys. They turn any waste food or drink that we don't need, or can't use as raw materials to feed our body, into our pee.

Getting rid of waste helps to keep the chemical balance of our blood correct (chemical balance sounds important, right?). When our blood chemicals are balanced, we are more likely to FEEL more balanced and so better in our heads.

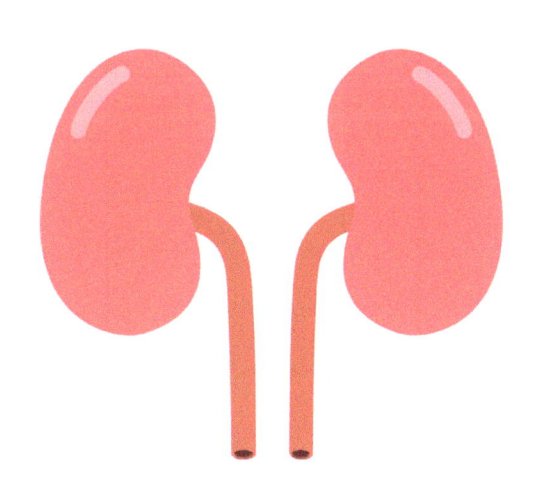

Bladder

Our bladder is like a balloon – it stretches to store our pee. 🎈

Then, when we are ready (that is, in the bathroom! 😝), it is like a muscle that contracts to push our pee out.

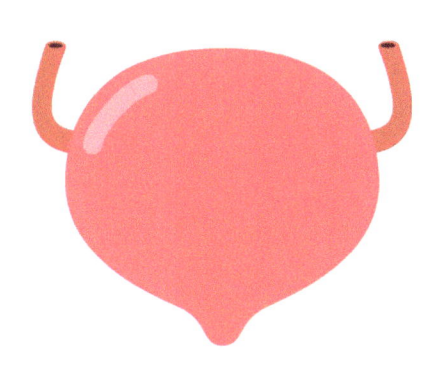

Heart

Our heart is a muscle that pumps our blood through our blood vessels and all around our body. 💓

This brings the oxygen from our lungs, and vitamins and minerals from our food to all of our cells, which really need them to work well.

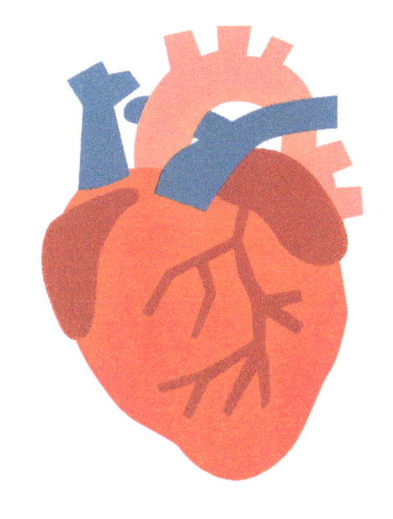

Stomach

Our stomach is the second place where our food goes after we swallow it. The first is, of course, our mouth – and did you know that our saliva contains digestive enzymes? Digestive enzymes (en-zimes) take the food apart so that the fibre, vitamins and minerals mixed up with other things, like sugar, can be separated out to be digested later. So, we really should chew our food well to let them do their work. Otherwise, they are standing around with nothing to do, getting bored, and we can't have that! If our food arrives in our stomach without being chewed properly, our stomach acid and enzymes are not very happy because it gives them more work to do!

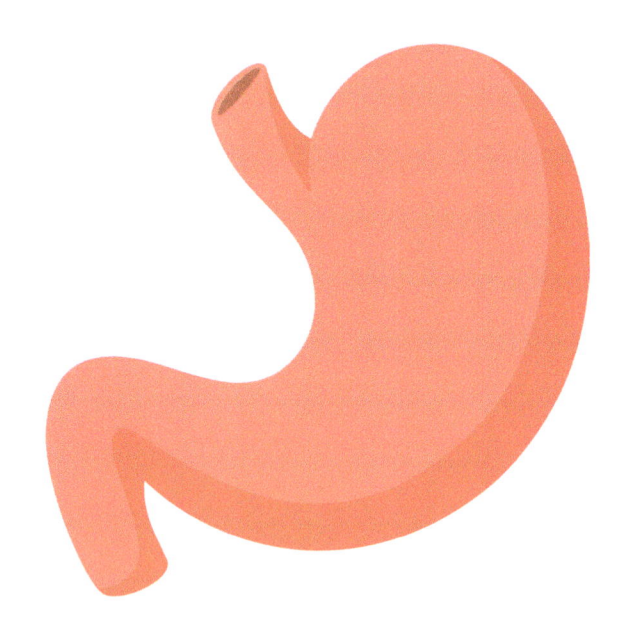

Our stomach is like a bag, and it contains acid and digestive enzymes.

It is also like a muscle because it churns the food around so that the acid and enzymes can mix with every single piece of food. Do you know what a cement mixer looks like? Well, your stomach is a little like a cement mixer.

Your food should be more like a liquid before it moves any further into your digestive system.

Then the vitamins and minerals (that is, the raw materials to help you to grow and think and basically work properly) can be used.

Small Intestine

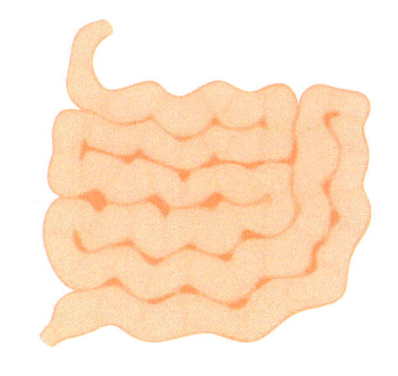

This is the next place that the food travels to after the stomach. Here, most of the goodness from your food is moved into your blood, which then brings the vitamins and minerals all around your body. This is really long and can be up to 22 feet in adults. Wow, isn't it hard to believe that a long tube like that is curled up inside your tummy? How amazing is that?!

Large Intestine

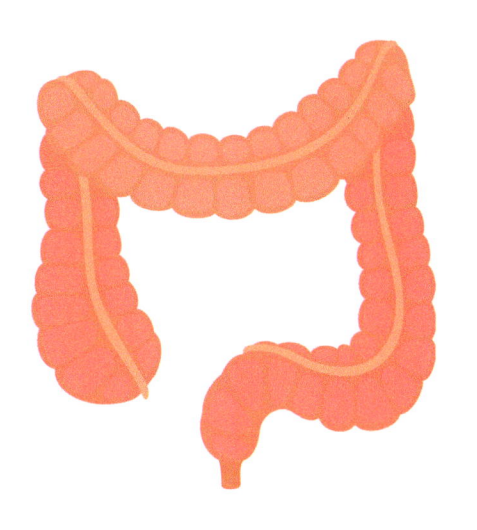

The next part is called the Large Intestine because it is wider than the small intestine. It is up to 5 feet long. Anyway, this is where your water is absorbed and also where the waste made by the liver goes to, to get ready to be excreted (x-cree-ted) – did someone say poop?!

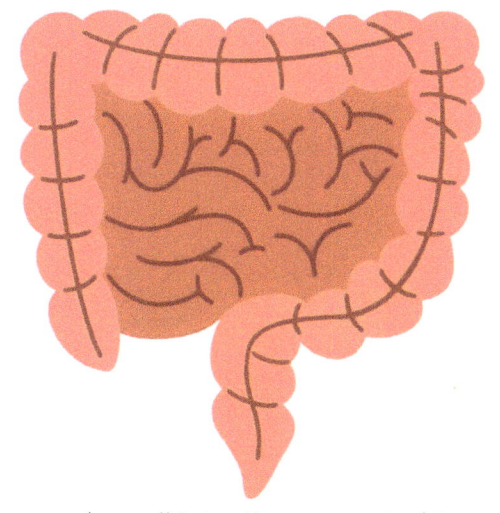

Large and small intestine snuggled together

Skin

The skin is our largest organ and obviously covers our whole body. That means that it covers all of our other organs to protect them from the outside, and I guess from falling out – can you imagine!!! 🤪

It also helps to control our temperature. For example, if we are too hot, we will sweat a lot which helps to bring our temperature back down. 🥵

When we are in the sun, skin absorbs vitamin D, which is important for our bones and our mood.

We have a lot of nerves in our skin, and they tell our brain when we touch something, if it is hot or cold, or what something feels like.

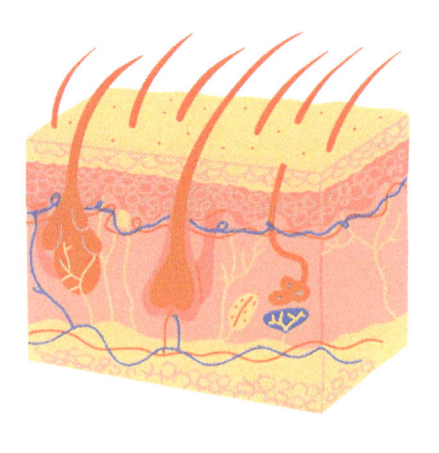

So, why do we need to eat food?

We feed our body with food, which should be full of goodness (nutrients), and this is our fuel, in the same way that petrol and diesel fuel our cars, or top-ups let us use our phones! When we get hungry, that is our body telling us that we need to top up! You wouldn't expect your phone to work without electricity, so it's the same for our whole body. If we want to feel physically and mentally strong, we need to eat good whole food (with the odd treat!)

NATHAN SAYS:
After learning about our organs, I think that the most interesting facts were that our skin absorbs vitamin D when we are in the sun, and our nerves will tell our brain if something is hot or cold and what it feels like!

Quick Quiz...

Which organ is like a balloon? _____

Which organ is like a cement mixer? _____

Which organ cleans our blood? _____

Which organ pumps our blood? _____

Which organ gets rid of carbon dioxide? _____

Name one organ that we have two of. _____

Which is our largest organ? _____

Where does food go after the stomach? _____

Where is water absorbed? _____

Which organ absorbs Vitamin D? _____

Where would you find most acid and digestive enzymes?

_____

Where does most of your food get absorbed?

_____

> **NATHAN SAYS:**
> *I think I need to read back over that section again, as I didn't get them all right!*

A Little Bit About Our Fuel, i.e. Food

What is a Nutrient (New-Tree-Ent)?

These are found in food, and we need them to grow, have energy and fuel our (billions of) cells to do all of the things that they need to do, so that we can breathe, walk, talk, listen, run, learn, feel happy and play. You might know them as minerals (not the same as fizzy drinks), vitamins, fibre, protein, healthy fats and carbohydrates.

Quick Quiz...

Without looking at the next pages, can you name 3 things that eating food does for us?

_____

_____

_____

Types of Nutrients and What They Do

Carbohydrates

Carbohydrates give us fuel for energy ⛽. We definitely need that for doing our homework and for playing sports. You need energy for computer games too, even though you are sitting down when you are playing them! I mean, your brain needs energy for all of the amazing work that it does and remember that we mentioned co-ordination earlier? I am no gamer, but I am pretty sure that you need to react very quickly when you are playing computer games, and your hands need to react to what your eyes are seeing.

> **NATHAN SAYS:**
> *You definitely do!*

Healthy Fats

We only need small amounts, but they are really important, and they can be used for fuel too. They help us to use vitamins, give us energy, protect our organs and keep us warm!☀️ Also, they are like raw material to make our hormones (chemicals which bring messages from our brain to, for example, our muscles to tell them to move or from our nerves in our skin back to our brain when we touch something). 🇪 You might have heard about omega-3. Well, this is an example of a healthy fat, and oily fish like salmon, mackerel and sardines are great sources. Walnuts (don't they look like a brain?), flaxseeds and chia seeds are plant sources.

Protein

Protein repairs and rebuilds our cells 🏗️ and so we need it to grow and keep our new cells healthy. It contains amino (ameeno) acids which cause important chemical reactions in our bodies.

Fibre

Fibre keeps our food moving through our body and makes sure that we poop every day! Yes, I said EVERY day 💩.

Vitamins and Minerals

These are food for our cells 😋 There are a lot of vitamins and minerals, and they all help our cells to do different things, which is why we need to eat a variety of different coloured food. If you eat a variety of colours of fruit and vegetables, you will be eating a wide variety of vitamins and minerals – we will go through what they could be soon. When you get to that section, you can highlight the fruit and vegetables that you like and see if you are missing any colours!

Water

If you have flowers or plants at home, you know that you need to water them regularly, or they will not grow. Well, it is the same for our body. We need water so that everything works properly on the inside. It helps our blood to flow better, and we feel like we have more energy, too, when we are hydrated. 🌊

Quick Quiz...

Which type of food is raw material for hormones?
_____

What helps our blood to flow?
_____

What type of food is raw material to repair and build?
_____

Nearly ready to talk about food!

We just have to mention this first...

Breathing.

> **NATHAN SAYS:**
> *Eh, I'm doing it right now!!! What could we need to know about breathing?*

I know that you are thinking the same as Nathan, "Breathing, you say? Well, Lyn, we all know how to do that, silly!"

Hmm, or do we...

Thankfully, our brain makes sure that we breathe in and out automatically so that we stay alive (quite important, don't you think?) However, when we are busy or feel worried or anxious, or are over-thinking things in our head, we are in "fight or flight" state and our tummy is not working as well as it could.

In order to make the most of our food and the goodness inside it, we need to be in "rest and digest" state, when our tummy can do its job much better. We can get back into this state by taking a deep, slow breath and then breathing out for as long as we can, until our lungs are fully empty, before we breathe in again.

It is a really good idea to do this before we eat! Just take a deep breath before your meals and relax...

Breathing deeply can also make us feel better if we are feeling a little worried or anxious. If you ever feel as though you need to calm down because you are panicking or just want to feel better, these are two exercises that you can do to help you...

Left Nostril Breathing

Close over your right nostril so that you are breathing through your left nostril only

- Breathe in slowly to count of five
- Hold to count of five
- Breathe out slowly to count of five
- Do this five times

5-4-3-2-1

- Name 5 things you can see
- Name 4 things you can feel
- Name 3 things you can hear
- Name 2 things you can smell
- Name 1 thing you can taste

These exercises won't make things that are bothering you magically disappear, but they will hopefully help you to be able to deal with them better or feel calm enough to ask for help if you need it. We should never feel bad about asking for help from someone we trust. Getting back into rest and digest will also help your body to be able to make the most use of your food as well, which will help your nervous system. Helping, or supporting, your nervous system helps you to cope better with upsetting things that are happening.

So, tell us about food!

Actually, two more things...

...Because we're going to talk about water first! We briefly mentioned it a few pages ago (do you remember?), and we just wanted to tell you now, why it is so important to drink 6 glasses of water every day.

Can you remember one reason from earlier in the book why water is important?

_____

Well, there are actually a few good reasons why you should make sure to drink water throughout the day.

You probably know that you have a thermostat at home to control the heating. Water helps to control the temperature in your body when you get too hot or have a fever.

Did you know that sweat is made up of 99% water?

It helps your joints to move better (like oil in a car)

It delivers raw material from food to your cells and so keeps them working properly.

It helps you to sleep better, and sleeping well helps you to stay in a good mood.

It helps your brain to work better. If you ever think that you just can't sit down to do your homework, try drinking a glass of water and see if your brain works better. A deep breath can help as well.

If you ever feel tired during the day, try drinking a glass of water and see if you feel a bit better and have more energy. We'll bet you will!

If you ever get a headache, try drinking a glass of water because that can be a sign that you are dehydrated.

You may be likely to get irritated when you are told that it is time to switch off your phone, tablet or game console. Try drinking a glass of water before you complain and argue (which, let's face it, isn't going to get you anywhere anyway except into more trouble 😂). See if that helps to avoid an argument. Oh, and take a few deep breaths. Do you still feel quite so irritable?

> **NATHAN SAYS:**
> *I knew water was important, but I didn't know it was THAT important!*
> *I love drinking water anyway, especially after playing football, so that won't be a problem for me! I'll count how many glasses I have tomorrow to make sure I am drinking enough. Maybe you could do the same?*

And the last thing... Sleep

- Do you go to bed too late?

- Do you stay on your phone or tablet right up until you go to bed?

- Worse still – bring your phone to bed? Aaaagh!!!

If any of the above are true, you might need to rethink your bedtime routine, because you are missing out on the benefits of a good night's sleep!

Here's what happens when we don't sleep well a lot of the time:

- We get anxious, which does not help us to feel happy with ourselves.

- We get angry, which can mean that we fight with our family or friends.

- Our brain doesn't work as well in class or doing homework, which means that we might not do as well in school as we could.

This is what happens when we do sleep well regularly:

- We repair our cells so that we don't get sick easily.

- We grow new cells so that we can grow and replace old cells.

- Our detoxification (think of the bin lorry coming around to pick up your rubbish and recycling) system cleans out anything that we don't need from our body and our brain.

- Our brain files away things that happened and sorts them out so that we can wake up feeling better the next day.

Here are some tips:

- Put your phone or tablet away 2 hours before bed.

- Do not bring them into your bedroom.

- Sleep in a really dark room, so make sure your curtains are pulled over.

If you are afraid to go to sleep in the dark, ask your adults to switch off the lights when they come upstairs so that you can stay asleep and the light won't wake you up later.

Relax and have a chat with your family before going to bed. Try to think of something to laugh about with them from your day or from a TV or YouTube show.

Our body and brain work better when we get a good night's sleep, so we enjoy the fun times more and can deal with the tough times better.

> **NATHAN SAYS:**
> *Well, I'm not too bad with my phone, but YouTube could be a problem! However, I want to stay healthy, so I'm definitely going to try those tips.*

And Now Actually About the Food!

Fruit and Vegetables

It is important to eat a lot of colours or rainbow of fruit and vegetables, because all of the colours give our bodies (us) different nutrients or raw materials so that we can work properly (kind of like how your parents' cars need water, oil, fuel, brake fluid, windscreen wash, etc., to get you where you need to go).

They also contain phytonutrients (Fight-O-New-Tree-Ents), which help prevent damage to your body. Let's learn about each colour...

GREEN

Can you name 3 green fruits?

_____

_____

_____

Why green is Good:

- Eye health (and we really appreciate being able to see our family, friends and this lovely world, don't we? We also want to read and play sports and video games as well, so our eyes are very important)

- The function of our arteries (vessels or tubes which transport blood from our hearts all around our body – *yikes*, that's very important, so I guess we need to make sure that they are working well)

- Lung health (Gosh, breathing is so necessary, or we might go blue in the face. Eat greens to avoid going blue!)

- Liver function (Our livers are our biggest internal organ, it sits above our stomach and carries out about 500 functions – Yes, I said five hundred – How busy is that!)

- Cell health (We are made up of billions of cells!!! Healthy cells make up healthy organs – remember we talked about footballers being like cells and the team being like an organ? If each footballer is healthy, the team is stronger)

- Helping us to heal when we get hurt (Don't tell me that you have never tripped over (Oof!), banged into something (Ouch!) or fallen off something (Aaah!) because I won't believe you 😜, so never mind Iron Man or Wonder Woman, we need a healing superpower, don't we?

- Keeping our gums healthy (and without gums, we would have no teeth – can you imagine!!! 😨

> **NATHAN SAYS:**
> *It is okay not to like them all. Even if you eat a few, that is good as well. My favourites are apples, grapes and green beans.*

List and Images of some green fruit and vegetables

VEGETABLES		
Broccoli	Kale	Cabbage
Brussels Sprouts	Asparagus	Green Beans
Cucumber	Celery	Lettuce (& Other salad leaves)
Artichoke	Courgette	Spinach

FRUIT		
Kiwi	Green Apples	Green Grapes
Honeydew Melon	Limes	Avocado

Quick Quiz...

WHITE

Without looking at the next pages, can you name 2 white vegetables and fruits?

Can you name 2 white vegetables?

_____

Can you name 2 white fruits?

_____

_____

Why white is good:

- Bone health (So our bones help keep us upright, and without them, we would fall over and have to slither around the place like a snake 🤣 Can you just imagine)

- Blood flow (Our blood delivers our nutrients and oxygen around our body like the ESB delivers electricity to our houses so that we can turn on lights and heat and even more important...the internet!!! When there is a storm, and the ESB goes off, it is a bit of a nuisance, isn't it? Well, we need our blood to keep flowing properly so that everything can work for us properly too)

- White vegetables help our arterial (R-teer-e-al) function. Our arteries are like pipes that bring blood into an organ, and they need to be clean and not clogged up, or else the whole thing would slow down.

- They help to keep our immune system healthy so that we can prevent illness (our immune system is like our own personal army, which protects us from illness and infection. When something gets into our body that is going to cause us harm, our army fights it off to keep us well 🎖️ Did you know that you had your own agents of shield superheroes right there inside you? Most of them are in your tummy as well, which is why you need to feed them the right food to keep them healthy.

List and images of some white fruit and vegetables

VEGETABLES		
Onions	Cauliflower	Mushrooms
Garlic	Leeks	Ginger
Potatoes	Parsnips	Fennel

FRUIT		
Pears	Dragon fruit	White lychee

> **NATHAN SAYS:**
> *The only white vegetable I've had before is a potato, so I must try some new ones. I think I will try mushrooms next.*

YELLOW and ORANGE

Without looking at the next pages, can you name 3 orange vegetables and fruit?

Can you name 3 yellow or orange vegetables?

_____

_____

_____

Can you name 3 yellow or orange fruits?

_____

_____

_____

Why orange and yellow are good:

- Eye health (As we said earlier, our eyes come in really handy!) 👀

- Growth (We are all different heights and sizes and shapes, and that is perfectly fine because we are all perfect being different and ourselves. However, we are all growing new cells all of the time, and we want them to be healthy new cells. You know, for example, when you fall over and cut your knee? You need to grow new skin then too.

- Immune system (your own army of soldiers that we talked about before in the white vegetables section, love orange and yellow vegetables too!)

List and images of some yellow and orange fruit and vegetables

VEGETABLES		
Yellow Tomatoes	Yellow Peppers	Yellow Beets
Carrots	Orange Peppers	Pumpkin
Butternut Squash	Sweet Potato	Corn

FRUIT		
Lemons	Oranges	Peaches
Nectarines	Tangarines & Satsumas	Mango
Pineapple	Bananas	Yellow Pears
Melons	Yellow Apples	Apricots

NATHAN SAYS:
I did really well on this quiz because yellow and orange are my favourites! I love pineapple, oranges, lemons, mango, yellow peppers and carrots. I'm so glad I like them because they are good for my immune system.

RED

Without looking at the next pages, can you name 3 red vegetables and fruit?

Can you name 3 red vegetables?

_____

_____

_____

Can you name 3 red fruits?

_____

_____

_____

Why Red is good:

- Helps protect against illnesses because they have very strong anti-oxidants. (An-tee-ox-ih-dants) fight damage to our cells, and so they are very important to make sure that all new cells that grow are healthy.

- Helps our urinary (Your-In-Air-Ee) system, which helps us to pee!! (Eh, if I'm not mistaken, that is very necessary, and we want it to be healthy.)

List and images of some red fruit and vegetables

VEGETABLES		
Red Cabbage	Red Peppers	Radishes
Tomatoes	Red Onion	Rhubarb

FRUIT		
Red apples	Cranberries	Pomegranate
Red Grapes	Pink Grapefruit	Cherries
Watermelon	Raspberries	Strawberries

> **NATHAN SAYS:**
> *Well, I like red peppers, red apples, red grapes, watermelon and raspberries and strawberries. I love putting the berries into my smoothies, especially raspberries.*

PURPLE and BLUE

Without looking at the next pages, can you name 2 purple vegetables and fruit?

Can you name 2 purple or blue vegetables?

_____

_____

_____

Can you name 2 purple or blue fruits?

_____

_____

_____

Why purple and blue are good:

- Heart health (Our hearts are very important to pump our blood around our body)

- Brain (We need our brains for everything we do, not just school work – without us even thinking about it, our brain tells our muscles when to move, our lungs to breathe, our heart to pump, and many other things – isn't that amazing! It also helps us to remember things, so definitely comes in handy for homework too)

- Bones (Remember the slithery snake we mentioned earlier? We definitely need our bones to be strong)

- Arteries are big blood vessels, so they are like tunnels that cars and lorries go through. If they get blocked, then there is a traffic jam!

- Helps our immune system (aka) *The Avengers* fight illness.

List and images of some purple and blue fruit and vegetables

VEGETABLES		
Aubergine	Purple Cabbage	Beetroots
Purple Carrots	Purple Lettuce	Radicchio

FRUIT

Plums	Purple Grapes	Blueberries
Blackberries	Passion Fruit	Blackcurrants
Raisins	Prunes	Figs

NATHAN SAYS:
Which is your favourite purple and blue fruit? Mine are grapes and blueberries. I didn't realise how important our immune system was. I think I'll try some more purple and blue fruits now because they will help my immune system out a little bit.

Quick Quiz...

Give one example of why green is good

_____

Give one example of why white is good

_____

Give one example of why orange is good

_____

Give one example of why red is good

_____

Give one example of why purple is good

_____

Let's Find Out About Nuts and Seeds

Nuts and seeds are very good for your health, but you might know some kids who are allergic to some nuts, for example, peanuts. Always be respectful if someone you know has an allergy, because it can be very serious for their health. Be sure to take care of them – don't eat nuts when you are playing with them or having your lunch with them. When you are having a party, it would be a really good idea to ask the kids you invite if they have any nut allergies. Wouldn't it be really nice if you planned your party food so that you did not include anything that anyone was allergic to? Then they wouldn't feel like the odd kid out! That would be very kind of you.

Anyway, back to nuts and seeds – we'll bet you know about peanut butter, but did you know that there are many more types of nuts and seeds in the world? They are very good for your heart and contain fibre (great for your tummy) and protein (which you need to repair your body at night when you sleep). They also help you to stay feeling full so that you don't eat too many sweets (I mean, you can have some, just not too many)

Can you name 3 types of nuts or seeds that are not peanuts?

_____

_____

_____

NATHAN SAYS:
I really enjoy eating nuts – they are very good for you, so that's why I eat them. Also, because they are very yummy! My favourites are cashews and walnuts. When I come to Lyn's house, I always raid her stash of cashews!

All nuts are good for your heart and muscles, and have fibre and protein. So, let's tell you about some that we like and about some other reasons they are especially good for.

TYPE OF NUT/ SEEDS	WHAT THEY ARE ESPECIALLY GOOD FOR
Almond	Skin, Immune System (your personal army), Eyes
Brazil	Immune system, Growth
Cashew	Shiny Hair, Bones, Happiness
Chia Seeds	Glowing Skin, Healthy Hair, Fighting Illness
Coconut	Coconut can help to fight bacteria and viruses and help you stay well and healthy

TYPE OF NUT/ SEEDS	WHAT THEY ARE ESPECIALLY GOOD FOR
Flaxseed	Glowing Skin, Healthy Hair, Fighting Illness
Hazelnut	Healthy Skin, Protects your cells from damage
Pecans	Healthy Skin and Hair
Pistachio	Gives you energy and helps your blood pressure (speed of blood travelling through your veins); good for your eyes
Pumpkin Seeds	Great for healing (you know, when you cut yourself or get a bruise)

TYPE OF NUT/ SEEDS	WHAT THEY ARE ESPECIALLY GOOD FOR
Sesame Seeds	Great for your bones and muscles
Sunflower Seeds	Great for skin and bones and memory, learning and brain development
Walnut	Brain and good mood

Now, you don't need to eat loads and loads of all of these to stay healthy. All you need to do is eat a couple of different ones every day, and you will be doing yourself a real favour!

Each time you get some pocket money, treat yourself to a different type of nut or seed to taste them all. Every week I buy a different type, and I put them into glass jars. Before I know it, I have a lot of different ones on my shelf. Then when I am going to work, I put a few of each into a smaller jar and take it with me for snacks.

Sometimes, I sprinkle them on salads or soup as well, but you will see some more ideas in the recipes section.

> **NATHAN SAYS:**
> *You know what, that's what I should start to do, and you should too.*

Have you heard about whole grains?

Whole grains are exactly what they say – grains that are whole and have not been changed too much in a factory. When food stays the same as it was when it was grown, it is natural, and so your body (which is also natural) can understand it and knows what to do with it.

As we mentioned at the beginning, when food is changed too much (or processed), your body gets confused and doesn't know where the food should go or what it is supposed to do (kind of like if you tried to play tennis without a racquet! Can you even imagine – sure, that would be just like playing donkey, throwing the ball to each other 😅 much slower and much harder work and definitely not tennis!

That is why you should eat whole grain (brown) bread instead of white.

Can you name 3 grains?

_____

_____

_____

> **NATHAN SAYS:**
> *I now understand why brown bread is more healthy than white, because brown bread is less processed, so our body knows how to use it.*

TYPE OF GRAINS	WHAT THEY ARE ESPECIALLY GOOD FOR
Oats	Oats are one of the healthiest grains on earth. They are also gluten-free and have loads of vitamins, minerals, fibre and anti-oxidants. They help keep your blood sugar balanced and keep your blood vessels clear.
Brown Rice	Great source of fibre, and it also has magnesium, which helps you to feel calm and relaxed.
Barley	Source of fibre and helps keep your blood vessels clean
Quinoa	Source of protein (re-build) and fibre (tummy) and also is gluten-free.
Buckwheat	Source of protein, fibre and energy!
Wholewheat	Source of protein and fibre, and keeps your blood sugars balanced.
Popcorn	Source of fibre, anti-oxidants; helps to keep your blood moving properly!

My favourite grain is oats, and I think that it is actually a superfood because of all of the things that you can make with it and because it is so easy to find and so good for you. It is very good for your tummy because of the fibre in it, and it helps your blood to flow properly.

Rice is another favourite, and of course, brown rice is the best for you. Some people prefer how white rice looks, but I suggest adding a spice called turmeric to brown rice because it is yellow and it looks tastier then! Turmeric is very good for you because it can help to calm down inflammation (in-fla-may-shun) in your body and you just need to add a teaspoon, so a small amount goes a long way.

Quinoa (keen-wah) and buckwheat groats are very healthy and are gluten-free in case you cannot eat gluten. They are great sources of plant protein which helps your body build and repair itself. They are very fast and easy to cook as well.

Popcorn is so much fun to make at home for movie nights and is very easy to cook too!

> **NATHAN SAYS:**
> *I love popcorn when I am watching movies, and I love making it so that we can watch it pop in the pan.*

And finally – beans, peas and lentils

There is a group of food called legumes (lay-gooms).

They include beans, peas and lentils – and who doesn't love beans on toast? Although, actually, now that I think of it, Nathan doesn't!

If you get a chance to try them, they are nice to have every now and then.

Can you name 3 types of legumes that are NOT in the title above? This one might be a bit harder, though.

_____

_____

_____

These foods are super for protein which is like raw material to repair your body and also to build your cells and help you grow strong. They are also full of fibre, which makes sure that you go to the toilet every day to do a number 2 💩 If you don't go to the toilet, you will feel more tired and less full of fun!

LIST OF COMMON LEGUMES

Chickpeas	Black Beans
Kidney Beans	Pinto Beans
Red Lentils	Cannellini Beans

LIST OF COMMON LEGUMES	
Green Lentils	Peas

> **NATHAN SAYS:**
> *I love having my peas every week with our roast dinner.*

And, can we learn how to use some of these foods ourselves?

Recipes

I have taught Nathan some simple recipes, most of which don't need any sharp knives and so are not dangerous, which your parents will be happy about! Although you should still be supervised, especially because some of the recipes need the use of a cooker. And if any chopping is needed, check with your responsible adults first. By the way, don't forget to clean up after yourself!

The most important thing is to have fun in the kitchen, and then you will look forward to cooking. When I have ingredients in the cupboard and am wondering what to do with them, I Google them. I am very grateful to the thousands of chefs who share their recipes online.

I have been making the recipes in this book for many years and cannot remember all of the original sources of inspiration. Generally, because I am coeliac, I would have to alter them to suit my gluten-free ingredients and my taste, so please don't be afraid to experiment in the kitchen. If you like music, put on your favourite songs, or better still, cook with your family or friends and enjoy tasting and sharing the food afterwards.

We would like to share these recipes with you now...

CHIA AND OATS PUDDING

This pudding is great for breakfast or a snack. You can make it at night, and it will be ready to eat the next morning. You can make two at a time, and they will last in the fridge for 2-3 days.

Split the following ingredients between 2 clean washed jam jars:

- ½ cup of oats
- 2 dessert spoons of chia seeds
- 1 mashed banana
- 1 cup liquid (milk, oat milk, coconut milk or almond milk)
- ½ cup berries (blueberries, blackberries or a mix of all)
- 2 teaspoons of sesame seeds

Mix well with a fork to combine all the ingredients, cover with the lid and leave in the fridge overnight. The Chia pudding will be ready by morning!

> **NATHAN SAYS:**
> *At first, I hesitated to try this, but once I tried it, I really liked it. It also made me a bit more open to trying other foods that I thought I didn't like.*

PORRIDGE

Oats are really good for your tummy and your central nervous system, so porridge is great for breakfast. However, when I was your age, I was not a fan! So, I tried making it with ingredients that I really like and found a way to make it nice and creamy. Now I love it and have it most mornings.

Ingredients (per person)

- ½ cup oats
- 1 cup of milk of your choice
- 1 dessertspoon of seeds (choose from flaxseeds, sesame seeds, sunflower seeds, pumpkin seeds)
- Handful of berries (choose from strawberries, blueberries, raspberries, blackberries)
- Drizzle of maple syrup or honey

Method

1. Put the oats and milk into a saucepan and leave to soak for at least ½ an hour. You could even leave them soaking overnight in the fridge. Soaking the oats means that the nutrients are more free for us to use and make it faster to cook and so creamier to eat!

2. Put the cooker on a low heat and simmer the porridge, stirring every minute or so.

3. It should only take about 4-5 minutes to cook.
4. Put the cooked porridge into a bowl and add the seeds, berries and maple syrup or honey.

FYI: The seeds add protein to help you to stay feeling full for longer

> **NATHAN SAYS:**
> *I think that porridge would be good for the winter because it is warm and maybe the chia pudding in the summer – what do you think?*

Very important note: If there is honey in any recipe, don't give them to your baby brother and sister if they are under 1 year of age because it is bad for their little tummies.

PANCAKES (GLUTEN AND DAIRY FREE)

Who doesn't LOVE pancakes?

Ingredients for Pancakes

- 130g self-raising gluten-free flour
- 1 Egg
- 1 tsp honey
- Squeeze of lemon juice
- 70-80 ml oat milk
- 1 tsp zest of lemon (optional)

Method

1. Mix the flour and egg well with a fork until it looks a little like breadcrumbs.
2. Add the milk slowly and keep mixing.
3. Add the honey and lemon juice.
4. Mix really well.
5. Spoon onto a medium heat pan and turn over when you see holes start to appear on the top of the pancake.

Nathan is brilliant at making these. If you feel brave enough, try flipping one!

> **NATHAN SAYS:**
> *Once, I flipped my pancake, and it got stuck on the ceiling! You might think that when you hear gluten-free pancakes, they won't be that nice, but in my opinion, they are the best pancakes I have ever tried.*

Very important note: If there is honey in any recipe, don't give them to your baby brother and sister if they are under 1 year of age because it is bad for their little tummies.

Also, if you are allergic to eggs, you can replace them by doing the following:

Mix 1 tablespoon of chia seeds with 3 tablespoons of water and leave this mixture to sit for about 10 minutes. When it has become "jelly-like", mix in with the flour instead of the egg.

OAT BREAD

Comforting, tasty and full of nutrients – good for your tummy, your heart and your concentration!

Ingredients

- 500g oats
- 20g GF flour
- 2tsp GF baking soda
- 500ml dairy-free yoghurt (Koko)
- 2tbsp oat milk
- 1dsp rapeseed Oil
- 1dsp honey
- ½ tsp salt

Method

1. Whizz oats in food processor to size of wheat meal.
2. Mix dry ingredients and then mix wet ingredients and stir.
3. Then combine both and mix well. Put mixture in a greased 2lb loaf tin and sprinkle with oats. Put in pre-heated oven at 180 deg C for 55-60 minutes. If not fully done, put back in for 5 minutes at a time, but 60 should do it (depending on your oven).
4. Leave in tin on wire rack for about 5 minutes, then remove carefully and cool bread on rack.

Eat it with some lovely butter and jam on top!

EGGS

Eggs are a great source of protein (raw materials for fixing things and growing). The protein is in the white part, and the yellow yolk has brilliant vitamins like Vitamin B12 and Choline which are great for our brain. Even if you think you can't cook, try any of these simple recipes because they are really easy. Another good thing about eggs is that they are nice for breakfast, lunch or tea-time! Because you need a cooker, check with your adult if you need help, because you do NOT want to burn yourself!! That would be kind of silly, not to mention really sore.

Boiled Eggs

This is the easiest way to cook eggs.

Method

1. Put some water in a saucepan (enough to cover the eggs), and with your adult nearby, pop it onto the cooker at high heat until the water is boiling.

2. If the eggs are at room temperature before you put them in the hot water (that means they are not cold from the fridge), the shell will be less likely to crack.

3. Then, very carefully with a spoon, put however many eggs you need into the boiling water (again, you might need some help with this)

4. Do you like them soft or hard? I like them soft if I am eating them warm, and I prefer them hard if I am eating them cold in a sandwich or on a salad.

So these are the times, depending on how you like them:

- Soft runny 5 minutes

- Medium runny 7 minutes

- Hard 10 minutes

You can do so many things with boiled eggs, and these are just a few ideas:

- Mash them and put them on toast or in a sandwich

- Crack the top (which is very satisfying) and scoop it off and then dip toast soldiers into it. When the yolk is finished, scoop out the lovely white part, which we mentioned is the part that has the protein

- If the shell has not broken, hard-boiled eggs will be safe in the fridge for up to 7 days, so they are handy to have as snacks or in salads, especially after sport (because they have protein)

Poached Eggs

Now my Mum makes the very best poached eggs, so they are real comfort food to me. They are also boiled, but without the shells. People have different tricks to make their perfect poached eggs, but I like to keep it simple.

Method

1. So the first step is to crack your raw eggs gently into a cup or bowl without breaking the yellow yolk.

2. Then, put some water into a saucepan and pop it onto the cooker at a high heat until it is boiling (with the help of an adult, of course – am I boring you repeating myself!!).

3. Once the water comes to the boil, make it swirl by moving a wooden spoon in a circle a few times and then let the eggs slide into the water gently.

4. The swirling action will help the whites to stay together with the yolk.

5. Then turn the heat down to medium or low – just high enough to keep the water simmering (that means not quite boiling, but you have a little movement at the top of the water).

6. If you like your eggs runny, leave them to simmer for 3 minutes and if you prefer them hard, about 5-6 minutes.

They are lovely with mashed avocado on wholegrain toast – yum!

Scrambled Eggs

These are delicious, but if you use the wrong saucepan, they can be very hard to clean up afterwards! I have a pan which is made from recycled materials and is non-stick: it is the best pan I ever had for making scrambled eggs and is the easiest to clean.

Ingredients

- 1-2 eggs per person
- Dash of milk
- Salt & Black Pepper

Method

1. Crack the eggs into a bowl.
2. Add a dash of milk and a tiny bit of salt and lots of black pepper.
3. With a fork, whisk the mixture until everything is combined and the yolk and white are completely mixed through.
4. Pop your pan onto the cooker (with the help of you know who) on a medium heat, and once it is warm, slowly slide the egg mixture onto the pan.
5. Use a spatula to very gently stir the eggs around the pan until they are all scrambled.

You could have them on wholegrain toast with some beans on the side.

OMELETTE

Omelettes are a bit like an eggy pancake, and you can add more vegetables to them (for example, spinach, peppers, courgettes) when you get used to making them. You would just have to cook the vegetables through a little first to make them softer because they take a little longer to cook than the eggs.

Ingredients

- 1 knob of butter
- 5-6 sundried tomatoes (or 2 cherry tomatoes)
- 1 tsp of dried parsley
- 2-3 eggs whisked
- 2 dessertspoons of grated cheese

Method

1. Heat the pan over a medium heat on the cooker.
2. Add ½ of the butter onto the pan and the tomatoes and parsley.
3. Turn the heat down to low and slowly add the whisked eggs to the pan.
4. Leave on the pan for 2 minutes, and then see if you can lift the sides (a bit like a pancake) with a spatula.
5. Then add the cheese to one half of the omelette and cook for another minute.

6. Turn off the heat, and then with the spatula, flip over the half without the cheese on top of the half with the cheese.

Slide it off the pan onto a plate and cut up into whatever size or shape you like.

If you had any fresh parsley, it would look nice to put a few leaves on top of the omelette on the plate. (Parsley contains vitamin C and zinc, too, and is very easy to grow at home in a pot on your window sill).

> **NATHAN SAYS:**
> *I am trying to eat more eggs because they have protein, and I need that because I am growing and training for soccer and Gaelic football. I haven't figured out my favourite egg recipe yet, but I think it is scrambled.*

COOKIES

These cookies are made with ground almonds instead of flour, and so they are gluten-free and a great source of protein!

Ingredients

- 2 cups of ground almonds
- 1/2 teaspoon of baking powder
- 1/8 a teaspoon of salt
- 1 teaspoon of vanilla extract
- 1/3 cup of maple syrup
- 1/3 cup of coconut oil melted
- 1/2 cup dried cranberries (you could substitute with some other dried fruit)
- 1/2 cup of chopped hazelnuts (or walnuts or cashews)
- 1 egg

Method

1. Pre-heat your oven to 200°C.
2. Combine the almonds, sea salt and baking powder in a bowl.
3. Separately combine the wet ingredients.

4. Mix the wet and dry ingredients together.
5. Finally, fold in the dried fruit and the chopped hazelnuts.
6. Spoon onto parchment paper and pop in the oven for 12 minutes.
7. However, check after 10 in case your oven is different. Enjoy!! 🤩😋

Storage

Store in an airtight container for up to 2 days. They also freeze really well.

> **NATHAN SAYS:**
> *These are the best cookies and have lots of protein in them because of the nuts, so they are good to eat after sports.*

FLAPJACKS/GRANOLA BARS

I have been making these granola bars for a long time now and can't remember where I got the recipe from, but it is a good one! When you find recipes online, don't be put off if you don't have all the exact ingredients in your cupboard. For example, you could use flaxseeds instead of chia seeds here.

- 3 tbsp maple syrup
- 1 tbsp chia seeds & 3 tbsp water
- 1 egg
- 1 tsp sea salt
- 50g desiccated coconut
- 2 tbsp coconut oil
- 40g chopped dried fruit
- 120g oats
- 50g chopped nuts

Method

1. Melt maple syrup and coconut oil gently in a pan and take off heat when melted.

2. In a small bowl, mix chia seeds and water well, and gel will form.

3. Mix this 1 tsp at a time with the syrup and oil.

4. Beat the egg and mix with the above (ensure mixture is not too warm, or eggs will scramble)

5. Add in fruit, salt, oats, coconut and nuts and mix really well.

6. Put mixture into a greased baking pan in pre-heated oven (150 deg C) for 25-30 minutes.

7. Press into a baking tray and refrigerate for at least 20 minutes.

8. Cut into 12 bars or roll before refrigerating.

IDEAS FOR SMOOTHIES

Really you can make a smoothie with whatever flavours you like, but these are a couple of ideas to get you started. You will need either a blender or a Nutribullet. They are a great way to get some vegetables and fruit into your day.

> **NATHAN SAYS:**
> *Mmmm! I love my smoothies, and they are an easy way to get fruit and vegetables.*

Super Strawberry Smoothie

- 3 strawberries
- 2 big spoons of yoghurt
- ½ banana
- Handful of cashew nuts (they are a soft type of nut, and so they will blend more easily and are a good source of protein. Do you remember why protein is good?)
- Cover with water and blitz while singing your favourite song until everything is like a liquid.
- Pour and enjoy.

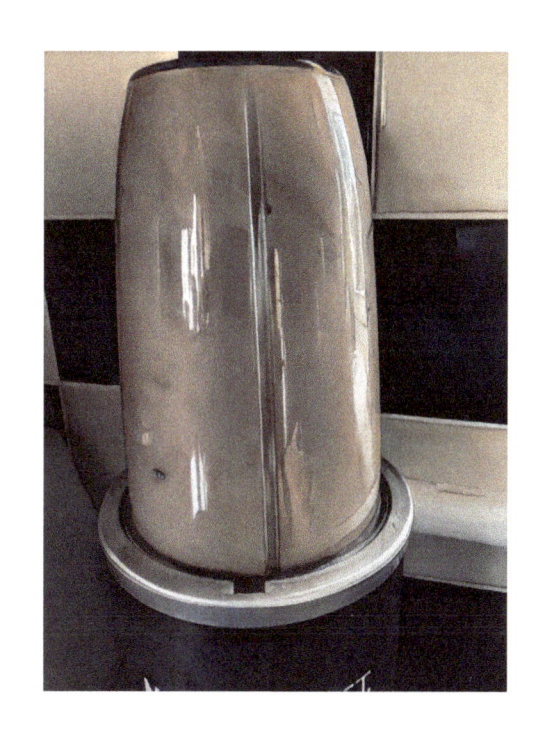

Gorgeous Green Smoothie

- Handful of spinach (I know – it's green! But you won't even taste it)
- 2 big spoons of yoghurt.
- About 8 pineapple chunks.
- Big tablespoon of flaxseeds or chia seeds.
- Cover with water and blitz while dancing like a puppet until everything is like a liquid.
- Pour and enjoy.

BAKED SWEET POTATO

Sweet Potatoes are very good for you and can you remember what the orange colour is good for? Have a guess and then go back and check.

Baking potatoes takes a little time, but they are so worth it!

Ingredients

- Sweet potato
- Rapeseed Oil

Method

1. Turn the oven on to 220C or 200C if you have a fan oven (check with your adult)
2. With a skewer (very carefully), prick the skin to make some holes in it.
3. Drizzle a little bit of oil over the potato or potatoes, and with a spoon, brush or your fingers, spread the oil over the skin.
4. Bake for 20 minutes (set the timer) and then turn the oven down to 190C or 170C (fan oven).

5. Bake for another 45 minutes, and then ask you know who to help you to check to see if it is soft on the inside by putting a skewer into it

6. If it is a bigger potato, it might need another 15 minutes or so.

When it is ready, with help, cut a cross in the skin and then add whatever you like to the centre (for example, butter, tuna, beans, coleslaw). You could also serve it with some salad leaves for green goodness. You could use a white potato instead.

> **NATHAN SAYS:**
> *What's not to like about a nice mushy spud?!*

PIZZA

Making pizzas at home is fun, and you can make them really colourful.

Ingredients

- Pizza Base
- Jar of passata
- Cheese

Any toppings you like (for example, peppers, ham, pepperoni, pineapple, rocket, sundried tomatoes)

Method

1. Smear passata on the pizza base with a spoon.
2. Add some grated cheese and then the toppings that you like.
3. Sprinkle some more grated cheese on top.
4. The times and temperature will be on the packaging of the pizza base so check that and pop your pizza in the oven at the right temperature.
5. Make it colourful!!

Little note – you could also use pitta breads to make little mini pizzas. Just put them in the toaster, and when they pop back up, leave them to cool for a minute or two. Then add the passata, cheese and toppings and melt the cheese under the grill (with some help because the grill will be hot)

NATHAN SAYS:
Now you are talking! It's a good idea to make pizzas a little healthier by making them at home.

PASTA SALAD JAR

These would be great for school lunches or for picnics! You can store them in big glass jars in the fridge, and they will keep for a few days.

Ingredients

- 4 dessertspoons of cooked pasta (you could ask your parents to cook extra if you are having it for dinner and then let it cool down)
- 4 dessertspoons of grated cheese
- 2 dessertspoons of mayonnaise

- 2 dessertspoons of natural yoghurt
- 2 dessertspoons of seeds (pumpkin, sunflower, sesame)
- 4 radishes
- 8 slices of cucumber
- 4 cherry tomatoes
- 8 strips of yellow pepper

Method

1. Mix the mayonnaise and natural yoghurt together.
2. Layer the ingredients between 2 glass jars, starting with the pasta.
3. Add the Mayonnaise and yoghurt dressing.
4. Add the vegetables in layers by colour.
5. Pop them in the fridge, and they will keep for two days.

You could use all sorts of vegetables that you like in this and also add chicken or tuna instead of the cheese. Play around with the colours: the good thing about using glass jars is that you can make the insides look like a rainbow. You can also either eat it from the jar or toss it out onto a plate and mix it all together. When you eat a colour rainbow of vegetables, you know that you are eating a good mix of vitamins and minerals to help keep you healthy.

> **NATHAN SAYS:**
> *I like pasta and most of the food in this list, but you could definitely put in whatever you like best, so this is a great idea for school lunches. Sometimes it would be nice to have something different to a sandwich.*

FRUIT SKEWERS

These are another good idea for your lunch box or a picnic. Pick different coloured fruit which don't need a knife, or if you have other fruit that you like, ask for some help to cut them up into the same size.

Ingredients

- Blueberries
- Pineapple
- Apples
- Satsuma Orange peeled

Method

1. Put a grape, then a strawberry, then a blueberry, then a piece of orange onto the skewer and keep going until the skewer is full.

2. You could dip the skewer in yoghurt before eating it.

3. Put the fruit pieces onto the skewer in whatever order you like to make it look nice.

> **NATHAN SAYS:**
> *This one is so easy! Different colours make food look nice, and when it looks nice, we want to eat it more.*

NUT-FREE DATE PROTEIN BALLS

These little balls are great to make because they don't need a cooker. They are fun and sweet but with all natural ingredients. This means that they are a better choice for your brain and your body than sweets or crisps (which, of course, you are going to have sometimes, just not every day!). They are sweet treats to don't eat too many all at once and share them with your friends and family.

Ingredients

- 1 ½ cups (200g) dates
- ½ cup of oats
- ½ cup of coconut chips
- ¼ cup of cacao
- ¼ cup of flaxseeds
- ¼ cup of mixed seeds (sesame/sunflower/pumpkin)
- Desiccated coconut

Method

1. Put all of the ingredients, except the desiccated coconut, into a food processor and mix until the mixture looks very well blended together.
2. Take the mixture out a spoonful at a time and roll into little balls or whatever size you like.
3. Roll in the desiccated coconut and place on a tray.
4. Put into the fridge for ½ an hour.
5. Store in a glass jar in the fridge.

> **NATHAN SAYS:**
> *I actually like these even though I hadn't tasted some of these ingredients before. They are just like sweets, really, but better.*

PEANUT BUTTER PROTEIN BALLS

Ingredients

- 1 cup of oats
- ½ cup of peanut butter (or almond or cashew butter)
- ¼ cup of honey
- ¼ cup of desiccated coconut
- ¼ cup chocolate chips
- ¼ cup of dried cranberries

Method

1. Put all of the ingredients into a bowl and mix really well with a wooden spoon.
2. Take a heaped dessertspoon of the mixture at a time and roll into ball shapes.
3. Put on a tray in the fridge to set.

Both of these protein balls are great for parties and lunch boxes, and you can make a big batch to store in the freezer in advance. You could mix in other ingredients that you like too. For example, little seeds, chopped nuts or mini marshmallows might be nice for a party.

Very important note: If there is honey in any recipe, don't give them to your baby brother and sister if they are under 1 year of age because it is bad for their little tummies.

DARK CHOCOLATE COVERED BERRIES

Anti-oxidants, omega-3 and vitamin C-rich treat.

Ingredients

- 2 dark chocolate bars (70% Cocoa or higher)
- 1 tablespoon toasted flaxseeds
- 1 tablespoon toasted sesame seeds
- Fresh blueberries, strawberries or raspberries

Method

1. Melt chocolate in a bowl over a pan of simmering water.
2. Stir frequently until melted and smooth.
3. Stir in the seeds.
4. Remove from the heat.
5. Mix in your berries.
6. Spoon clumps of mixture onto greaseproof paper on baking sheet.
7. Refrigerate until firm (approx. 10 minutes).

> **NATHAN SAYS:**
> *I really like these, and they are super-easy to make.*

POPCORN

1. Pour a little rapeseed or olive oil onto the bottom of a saucepan.

2. Cover the bottom of the pan with one layer of popcorn kernels.

3. Put on the lid.

4. Place on a medium heat.

5. When they start to pop, shake the saucepan every minute or so until all the kernels have popped.

6. You will have more popcorn than you thought!

7. Put in a big bowl and sprinkle over a little sea salt not too much).

> **NATHAN SAYS:**
> *We always make a big bowl of popcorn when we are watching movies together, and turn off the overhead lights, so it is like being in the cinema!*

If you or anyone else in your family would like some more recipes using natural foods, you can check out www.lynsharkeynutrition.ie/recipes

That's it from us!

Well, it's time to finish up, but we hope that you found some interesting facts in our book, and we really hope that you will try to eat more natural foods. Of course, you can still have some treats, but just not every day and please eat some vegetables!!! 😉. They will help you to grow.

If you eat more healthy food every day, you will have more energy, which will help you to feel better and enjoy your day better – it is as simple as that.❤️

The most important thing, however, is that you are happy with yourself, just the way you are. None of us are perfect, and believe it or not, everyone has bad days, even though it might not look like it from the outside. We all make mistakes. Go easy on yourself if things don't go right, and remember that tomorrow is another day.

Just be nice to yourself and to everyone you meet.

Have a wonderful day!

Lyn and Nathan 🙏⚽

Milton Keynes UK
Ingram Content Group UK Ltd.
UKHW050305191123
432820UK00006B/61